TELLING OF PARADISE

Ann with her beloved Cowslips on
downland at Lydden near Dover, May 1996

*The verse on the title page was composed by Ann in
January 1996 after the loss of her younger brother
Philip. She had added the words – 'Thoughts' directly
after dear little Philip's passing. The first two lines are
adapted from the well known hymn by Charles Wesley.*

TELLING
OF PARADISE

ANN CHICK

'Tis Love Divine
All Love's Excelling,
'Tis Love Beyond
All Human Telling.

First published in 2004 by
Warren Press
Ark Cottage
Sowell Street
St Peter's
Broadstairs
Kent CT10 2AT

ISBN 0 9547492 0 0

Printed and bound by
SMITH SETTLE PRINTING & BOOKBINDING LTD
Ilkley Road, Otley, West Yorkshire LS21 3JP

CONTENTS

Introduction   ix

1974

The Cloud of Night   3
Snares and Meshes   4

1975

Spring Awakening   5
To My Husband   6
I Would Have Cowslips   7

1976

Images of Earth   8
Tenuous Light   9

1980

Earth – I Love Thee   10

1984

We Shall Find Our Love Again   11
Wild Flowers Blew   12

1985

My Spirit Sings on Still   13
Wild Flowers   14
On Such a Day   16
The Lost Flower   17
There Comes Back a Loveliness   18

1986

Love Is   20
April Morning   21
The Blossoming Tree   22
Wild Geese   23
Mayflies   24
Treasure   26
I Thought That I Had Come to Gather Flowers   28
Against the Night   30

1987

They Cut the Tree Down   32
Paradise   34
Under the Summer Sun   35
Rose of Light   36
Mystical Roses   37
Bear With Us – Share With Us   38
Breath of My Breath   40

Two Suns   41
The Vision   42
I Know a Stream   44
Peace   45
1988
Love and Light   48
Anemones   49
Radiant Earth   50
Broken   51
White-Winged Bird   52
Brave Bird   53
In Time to Come   54
It is Night   55
The Blackbird's Song   56
The Light of Paradise   57
Luminous Butterflies   58
And Still I Love –   59
The Garden   60
Light   61
Eden – Long Ago   62
The Elephants   64
Candles in the Dark   65
Returning Spring   66
Storm's End   67
Soul Child   68
The Berried Tree   70
1989
Christmas Eve   74
Loss   75
The Sea Lavender   76
Golden Flowers   77
My Will, My Will   78
What Now Remains?   79
1990
It is Innocence   82
The Sweet Birds Sing   83
The Little Hawthorn Trees   84
The Sleeping World   85
The Trespassers   86
Moment of Roses – for Rosie   87
Soul's Country   88
Not of the Night   90

vi

Little Lizard   91
Morning Suns   92
1991
  I Was a Garden   96
  Elegy   97
  See the Spring   98
  Water of Life   99
  The Vanished Land   100
  The Mirrored Dream   101
  A Small Bird Sings   102
  Roundelay   103
1992
  Echoes   106
  Bringer of Gifts   107
  Is This the Place?   108
  Flowers of Light   109
  Fair Earth   110
  And I Shall Remain   111
  The Golden Land   112
  Storm Birds   113
1993
  Fire Bird   116
  Spring   117
  I Said to the Sun   118
  Dream   120
1994
  Innocence is Starlike   121
1995
  The World's Wound   122
  The Pheasants' Field   124
1996
  Innocence   125
1997
  Never such Light   126
1998
  Suspended Time   127
2001
  The Clouded Yellows   128
2003
  Love Is Eternal   129
  Acknowledgements   131

Ann in her much loved 'Brimstone Wood',
Yockletts Bank south of Canterbury, April 2000

INTRODUCTION

ANN passed from this life a little after midnight on Sunday the 20th of October 2002, her sixty third birthday. I can recall nothing of the subsequent bleak, dark drive home from the hospital in Canterbury to our home in Broadstairs except the determined resolve to see her poems in print.

We have always been extremely close spiritually, quite literally soul mates, and never in doubt about the continuation of our spirit selves. Ann's determination to establish contact with me following her passing, the quality of that communication in respect of her guidance and her concerns and love for me, as well as the reassurances of her continued well being, has allowed me a quiet peace which I could never have imagined possible and which has sustained me immeasurably.

Ann has always had a great love of poetry, and began to keep examples of her own work during the mid 1970's. A long period of her adult life was marked by emotional suffering. Possessed of a pure and deeply sensitive nature she was very vulnerable to the hurts of this often unkind world. She endured this with remarkable courage, great dignity and resolve. Nothing of this suffering diminished her and during a period in the 1980's when she unequivocally journeyed through the dark night of the soul, it was poetry, and the poetry which speaks from the soul and spirit, and touches the soul and spirit, that sustained and inspired her. It was this, together with our shared and eternal love and reverence for the natural world, which both slowly allowed back the light in her life and provided the impetus for her most productive period of writing.

Ann developed this love of the natural world from a very early age. Born on the Sussex coast during the early weeks of the second world war, she lived most of her life, over half a century, in Kent. However, most of the war years were spent with her family in Princes Risborough, surrounded by the peaceful countryside of rural Buckinghamshire. She never forgot her childhood memories of the joy and wonder of the wild flowers, insects and birds, and the beauty of that countryside. Cowslips particularly inspired a fascination that stayed with her all her life.

Ann possessed a wonderful, spiritual quality which was most firmly rooted in this contact with nature. The poems accompany her on an often difficult journey, providing a spiritual narrative, emphasizing the sense of her irrepressible joy of the natural world, and affirming her conviction of our spiritual oneness with the divine and of the divine presence in everything. There is a consistent and profound expression of this joy and she would often reflect that the words did not seem to come from her. Rare amongst us she had known the paradisal state in this life, both as a child, and for a time, during the early years of our married life. She had not drunk so deep as to have forgotten its promise and was always very aware of her spiritual identity.

In this life, she never sought to have any of her poems published and was always rather reluctant to agree whenever this was suggested. Happily, this is no longer the case. Since her passing she has expressed a great enthusiasm for them being more widely known and has emphasized that this is principally because she believes that they may help people. Ann has actively taken a spiritual hand in the publishing process and throughout has made changes and indicated her choices from a much larger body of work for the final selection. The request which was most challenging has been for me to produce the illustrations which accompany the poems. In the event this has proved most rewarding. All of these illustrations have some personal significance and treasured memory for both of us, and Ann has even suggested some subjects whilst rejecting others.

As her life became less stressful and more calm so her poems became less prolific with fewer than twenty representing her last ten years from 1992. However, the final period is dated 1992-2003. This is significant in the respect that the short, concluding poem was not written during her lifetime but received by me while in the early stages of preparation for this anthology, six months after her passing.

In a very real sense this book of poems has been a shared concept, not only with regard to the content but, significantly, its preparation.

We have known each other for most of our adult lives. We have journeyed together on a path that has often been far from easy but, reflecting the essence of much of Ann's poetry, never without the light of joy, wonder and love to illuminate our way. Without children, and because for all our married life I was able to work at home, we had much more time to share together. As we travelled through those many years, not only as marriage partners, but as friends and companions to the threshold of old age, we were always conscious of the brevity of this life and the certainty of the next.

One of my most constant and enduring memories of Ann in her earthly life has been her response to nature. The sight of any small creature or unexpected flower filled her with the innocent enthusiasm of a child. Now, her work done, she has returned to paradise. I know that when it is my time to return home, after this brief existence, I will be reunited with her in our happy fields, 'where joy for ever dwells.'

DEREK CHICK
October 2003

1970'S TO 1985

The Cloud of Night

O' lovely earth
From whose once fertile womb
All things had birth,
What have we done
To your radiant sun?

Vast vision
Veiled by invisible cloud
I cry aloud,
For now your perfect cloud
Has become our shroud.

O' lovely light
Now hangs above the earth
The cloud of night.

Snares and Meshes

Shall our raptures
Pass recapture
Shall our gains
Become as dust
Shall our eyes
Become unseeing
Children lose
Their quiet trust ?

That which gave us joy and rapture
All we know and all we trust
Now is caught in snares and meshes –
And eyes are blind
To the fair and just.

Spring Awakening

Today,
When clouds break
And when the warmed earth
Eases deep-buried creatures awake
And when in their lairs
Fur -covered creatures stir;
And when the sweet birds
Rise early to sing –
Then it's Spring !

To My Husband

My love,
Whose eyes are ever watchful
Who knows when sorrow
Shows in mine,
How much your presence
Gives life to me;
Your unspoken thoughts
Carry me through the darkness
Which comes often to me –
Out into fair fields of quietness.

There stand two trees –
The Oak, old in wisdom,
And strong of life's battles,
And the delicate Birch –
Whose slender stem
And airy branches
Have learned to bend
With comparative ease,
And join hands with you –
Whose sturdy roots
Enfold mine –
And keep strong –
Almost as yours.

I Would Have Cowslips

When I had cowslips in my hand
Full with flowers was our land,
My childish eyes could scarce contain
The brilliance of this shining main.

I sat for hours in sovereign reign
Over huge green seas washed clean by rain,
Full to bursting was my land –
When I had cowslips in my hand.

Now concrete blocks
Assault my eyes
Their multitudes
Blot out the skies;
My kingdom gone –
But had I planned
I would have cowslips
In my hand.

Images of Earth

Imprint on my mind
Your quiet shapes and sounds
The rich sweet smell
Of fertile ground
Your colours gold and green
Red, blue and deepest brown.

Let fall your essence
Down upon my eyes
Smooth now my brow
With hands of quietude;
Open my mind
To the high sweet cry of birds
Borne by the wind
Towards infinite skies.

Imprint again forever on my mind
Your loveliest of lovely
Shapes and sounds;
Of colours, scents and every
Singing-sound;
Of quiet blessedness
And thoughts profound.

Tenuous Light

This our earth
Was once a blessed place
All abundance
Full of quiet grace;
But we who plundered
Took away the sight,
Stand now with empty hands,
Confounded by our might.

Such a gloom there is
That shadows all our suns
To nothing,
And where ever we look
To find –
There is a chasm;
Such finality.
And yet this void
Was never meant to be.

Our days could shine
Like child's eyes again.
Our love once more
Could open flowers,
Fill gradually dark corners
Slip here and there
Upon the air,
And lull the heavy-eyed:
Lift gently lids
Long closed in quiet despair.

Could it be so ?
It must
Or thin fingers
Grasping tenuous threads
Of light
Will wither now
Amid the clamour
And the darkness
Of our night.

Earth — I Love Thee

Earth, I love thee
In every part of thee
Thy form adorned or naked —
Fair thou art
And clothed in loveliness to me.

Man's hand has touched thee grossly
Scarred deeply thy symmetry,
Thy sweetness
He has steeped in poison,
Measured with vulgarity.

I still love thee,
Bless thee for thy
Abundant generosity;
Giver, giver of each man's immortality
Why then
Shall we blast thee
Into dark infinity ?

We Shall Find Our Love Again

We shall see the sunlight
Where now all shadows seem,
And we shall find the rarest flowers
Where now rank weeds are seen.

And we shall hear the songs of birds
Where weeps now leaf and tree,
And we shall feel the softest showers
Blessing you and me.

And we shall walk in brighter fields
In a lighter, brighter sun,
And we shall feel a lighter peace
Than here, where we found none.

And we shall find our love again
Under a milk-white stone,
Shaded by the peaceful trees,
Protected by the sun.

The breath of flowers shall blow away
All shadows from our sun
The lightest, brightest field we'll find
And live again –
As one.

So place your hand again, my love
Within the hand of mine,
And by the sweetest Grace we'll find –
The Rose, the Tree, the Vine.

Wild Flowers Blew

When I walk through rich and ancient pastures
And golden meadows measureless in time
My heart is sad for this fair land's lost treasures –
And knows it now never can be glad.

And when I walk by streams and quiet waters
Down lanes with country names
Past cottages 'of flowers',
And see the harsh reality of urban life –
Its density –
I remember sadly –
That this is where, once,
Wild flowers blew.

And when I see the moving mass of vast humanity
And hear its din – deafening,
I look beyond
At spare trees and sky
Remembering –
That this is where, once
Wild flowers blew.

For now no shining poppies blow
Or flowers few,
No bird of light ascends to heaven's roof
Its golden song ringing, then descending,
As quietly as dew:
But fairest fields are quietly remembering –
That once, a time ago,
Wild flowers blew.

My Spirit Sings on Still

My sweet soul
From whom all innocence
Has fled
How fare you now ?

My soul replies:

'My spirit sings on still
Amid the wide clear skies;
It smiles on roses,
Sheds its tears
Upon the wings of butterflies
And chatters with the ever-singing birds;
It whispers quietly
Amidst the highest trees
And then takes flight
On vivid wings and sings
Midst Heaven's murmurings'.

Wild Flowers

See the wild flowers there
Observe their delicacy
Perceive how fair,
Years ago
Many blew there
All as lovely
All as fair,
Bloomed and shone
And scented the air
Blest the spirits
Passing there.

By their beauty
Some were saved
Hearts grew stronger
Souls more brave
Spirits weary
Walked again
As all the flowers
Shone -
Through their rain.

Numerous people
Passed them by
Plucked a bloom
And let it die
Plucked a bloom
And let it lie
Withering
Under the summer's sky.

Blooms lie broken
Withered and dry
Under the lovely
Summer's sky
Delicate petals
Desolate there
Bravely scenting
The summer air.

Now sleep the flowers
Brave and strong
Singing somewhere
A sweeter song,
Touching hearts
Of better men
Telling them
To love again.

On Such a Day

On such a day as this –
When Earth to Heaven
Bares its soul to kiss
That vast mysteriousness,

On such a day –
Sunlight streaming,
Bird-song teeming,
Flowers weaving
Tapestries;

On such a day
As this,
Bless Heaven's
Mysteries !

The Lost Flower

I had a flower in
My heart,
Once, a while ago –
A golden flower
Full and fair
Never had it any care,
Once, a time ago.

Now that flower's
Bloom has flown,
Withered petals,
No seed sown,
Empty, empty
Where it bloomed,
Aching sadness
For its tomb.

Had my flower
Sown a seed,
Somewhere safe
Among the weeds,
Happy would I then
Have been,
To know it bloomed
Again, unseen.

There Comes Back a Loveliness

When all life's dreams lie shattered
When all that I loved lies dead
When all that my soul believed in
Has vanished
Has perished
Has fled :-

There comes back a loveliness
To me
Of a bird that sleeps in a flower
Of a scent of blossoms like Heaven
Of a glory that shone
For an hour !

1986

Love Is

Love is Light
Love is Sun
Love is Two
Becoming One
Love is Gentle Tenderness
Love is Everlastingness.

Love is Fire
Love is Strong
Love's the Singer
And the Song –
Higher than my Soul
Can Fly
Shall I Know It
When I Die ?

Love is Pure
Shining, Bright,
Like a Ring of Perfect Light,
Love is Beauty
Undefiled
Love's Becoming
Like a Child.

Love is Not
For Those Who Dare
Never to Attain
The Fair
Never to Possess
The Prize –
For Love Demands
Love's Sacrifice.

April Morning

On this indelible day of Light –
Unparalleled by any made by Man,
Fly butterflies on emerald wings :
How my heart sings
To see their pure enamelling
Adorn, like some rare flower of spring,
The newborn leaves
Of the tender Hawthorn trees;
While all around
The sweet, fresh ground
Is gemmed with flowers of gold
And violet blue,
All shining and refreshed
By morning dew.

I kneel
Before this miracle of light and air,
What loveliness the earth now wears
For her Spring dress –
That every lilting bird
Shouts out with joy
And builds its nest;
Then folds its wings,
Acknowledging,
This Blessedness !

Written on hearing of the nuclear
disaster at Chernobyl in April 1986.

The Blossoming Tree

Come, my sweet one, sit with me,
Under the lovely Elder tree,
Here, beneath this blossoming tree,
Come, my dear one, watch with me.

Come, my dear one , come and see,
Beside this fragrant, blossoming tree,
All paradise prepared for thee
By the blossoming Elder tree.

Come, my dear one , watch with me,
See the wonder I can see,
All God's glory there for thee
By the blossoming Elder tree.

Sunlit river, gilded tree,
Singing song of bird and bee,
Dazzling flight of Bluebirds three,
By the blossoming Elder tree.

Soft the sun, beneath the tree,
Come, my dear one, rest with me,
Under branches cooling thee,
Come, my dear one, dwell with me.

Wild Geese

We sat you and I by a lonely stream
On a day full of light with a golden gleam
And we heard you and I in that beautiful sky
The echoing song that the wild geese cry :

Song of the wilderness, song of the snow,
Song of the wastelands from a time long ago –
Haunting and echoing, lonely and free,
Ancient as time and eternity.

Mayflies

Do you remember
When you and I
Watched the Mayflies
Like Fireflies
Soar into that
Pure Spring sky ?

Do you remember
That dazzling light
That touched their wings
As they took flight
And how they set
Our souls alight ?

Do you remember
You watched with me
Beneath that lovely
Fragrant tree
A-murmur with a
Cloud of bees
All feeding on its
Fragrant seeds
While sunlight gilded
The water reeds ?

Oh, I remember
That perfect light
And the lovely Mayflies
Bright Spring flight
And how they set
Our souls alight :

And how you quietly
Watched with me
Beneath that lovely
Fragrant tree
A-murmur with a
Cloud of bees
All feeding on its
Fragrant seeds
While sunlight gilded
The water-reeds —
And God fulfilled
Our every need :

Treasure

I treasure silence
Amidst the chaos
Of this now troubled world :
I love to hear
The leaves of trees unfurl,
And listen to that soft,
Unearthly sound
As a million flower petals
Are unwound.

I treasure Light
Amidst the blindness
Of this now darkened world :
I love to see that Shining -
As the storm clouds,
By that Light
Are hurled far back
To the vast hinterland
Of this so darkened world.

I treasure Beauty
In this now ugly world :
I love to see
The flights of birds
And hear their singing
Amidst all the flowering
Of the towering trees,
All murmuring with clouds
Of humming bees.

But most of all,
I treasure Love
Amidst the man-made lust
Of this now cruel world :
I see its presence
In the tender eyes
Of one I love,
And in the true compassion
Of the holy few
Who dedicate their lives
To me, and you.

I Thought That I Had Come to Gather Flowers

I thought that I had come to gather flowers,
To fill all my blossoming hours
With blessedness,
But with each bloom I gathered
I gathered sadness
Which broke
Like many petals
In my hand,
Scattering all their bright and broken
Loveliness
Upon the softly shining land.

Yet with each new and unasked for sadness
I planted in its place a fairer bloom,
And watched, through all the lengthening
Sunlit hours
Its climb from deep within
Earth's fertile womb,
Until its lovely face
It then unfolded,
To smile
And shed its ravishing perfume.

Then tenderly I touched its slender column,
And gazed, enraptured, on its Being fair,
And breathed, and caught and held
Its lovely fragrance,
Before it vanished soft
Upon the air.

I could not ever keep
Its lovely fragrance,
I could not ever keep
Its Being fair;
For I could only ever
Touch its shadow,
And only keep its image
In my care.

No, I could never keep or hold
Its Beauty,
I could not ever keep it for my own;
What now I know
Through all my darkening hours,
Belongs to all the smiling gods –
Alone.

Against the Night

Against the odds
And all the wishes of unsmiling gods
My spirit soared –
Made its escape
Through all of earth's
Interminable prison bars
And sang with stars.

Against the night
And all the darkness
That shuts out the light
My soul took flight
And sang –
Amidst the beauty
Of God's brightest lights -
Against the night –
And all the darkness
That shuts out the light.

1987

They Cut the Tree Down

Today,
They cut the tree, cut her in two;
While the birds in bewilderment clouded the blue;
Limb after limb fell severed and dead,
They cut the tree down,
They severed her head.

They severed her head
Once so tall and so proud
That her close-tendrilled locks
Blossomed in cloud;
In cloud and in sunlight
She blossomed anew
Unfurling her flowers
Of the tenderest hue.

Her leave-laden branches were bowers for birds
To sleep in, to love in
To build undisturbed
Their beautiful nests for their delicate eggs,
To the tree they entrusted their young
Till they fledged:
Till they fledged and they flew
Their first breathtaking flight
And returned full of joy
To sleep safe through the night.

But they cut their tree, cut their tree,
Cut her in two
While the birds beat their wings
And cried in the blue
Of the hole in the sky
Of the void in the air
And of all the bright beauty that shone in her hair.

A little tribute on the eventual felling of our
beloved Sycamore – after a long fight of a
dozen years to keep her.

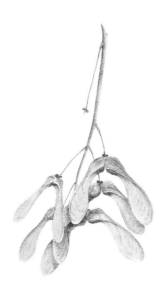

Paradise

I remember when the earth was clothed in flowers,
When all about me Heaven breathed delight,
When dandelions and daisies danced around me
Amid the fragrant grass like pure light.

And I remember when that dazzling light embraced me
And dressed me in a gown of pure white-
And when with precious perfumes it enrobed me
In innocence, all spotless, all delight.

Then I remember when I grew and blossomed
How some fair grace returned me to that land
When Heaven once again with joy enclosed me
And let me wander in her holy land :

Such vivid light
Such singing all around me
Such fragrance blown
By flowers all of light
Such happiness
Such ecstasy enclosed me
Such loveliness
That dazzled my pure sight.

For one brief moment I again was welcomed
Was clothed again in innocence and grace
For in that radiant light that shone around me
I caught a glimpse of Heaven's wondrous face.

— *The Kingdom of Heaven is Within You,*
  That's why I lived it !

Under the Summer Sun

Under the summer sun
Under the leaves
Lies the sweet Blackbird's nest –
Where she's at ease.

Under her downy breast
Under her wings,
Safe in their shadowy nest –
New life, sings !

Rose of Light

All that summer
Shone the roses
With a light
That love discloses
In the radiance
Of the roses.

Such a light
Of love reposes
In the radiance
Of the roses
Such a sweetness
Now uncloses
From the radiance
Of the roses.

Yes, all that summer
Shone the roses
Shone the light
That love discloses
Breathed the sweetness
From the roses
Of the light
Where love reposes.

Mystical Roses

Mystical roses
Mirrors of light
Radiant reflections
Of a wondrous sight,

Matchless of flowers
Immaculate there
Fragrant with sunlight
And rain-warm air,

Memorable roses
Fragrant with love
Lit by the lustre
Of stars high above,

Petalled with tenderness
Softer than air
Mirrors of beauty
Beyond compare.

Bear With Us – Share With Us

Bear with us
Share with us
Share in our loss
Cry the crucified creatures
Now nailed to the cross –
Now nailed to the cross
By man's greed
By man's loss
In daring to think himself
Greater than God.

Bear with us
Share with us
Share in our pain
Cry the transparent tears
Of the crucified rain –
Of the crucified rain
Once as pure as God's breath
Now poisoned by man –
O' share in our death.

Bear with us
Share with us
Share in our grief
Cry all the great trees
With their desolate leaves,
As they fall like a pall
Over blossomless lands –
O' bear with us
Share with us –
Hold our small hands.

Yes, bear with us
Share with us
Share in our pain
Cry all the small creatures
On the wind and the rain:
Yes, bear with us
Share with us
Innocents all –
So gracefully bearing
The weight of man's fall.

Breath of My Breath

Breath of my breath,
Bone of my bone,
Flesh of my flesh,
By love finely honed.

Eye of my eye,
Tear of my tear,
Smile of my smile,
My soul you beguile.

Heart of my heart,
Mind of my mind,
Life of my life,
My most blessed find.

Calm of my calm,
Storm of my storm,
Dark of my darkness,
Shall we be re-born ?

Star of my star,
Light of my light,
Man of my maiden,
Live through our 'dark night'.

Two Suns

Now as we see
How swift the hours pass
We know ourselves to be
As insubstantial as glass;

And as fragile
And transparent
Mirroring each the other one
And both of us
A shining sun.

Ah, how bright
Did we become
Among the myriad other ones,
But now more wise
Now sands have run
For tiny were
Our shining suns.

Yet how bright
Though brief their span
Amid the boundless skies of man !

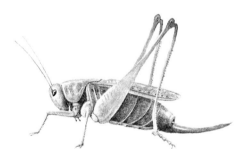

The Vision

I passed by fields
Of pure, unsullied fragrance,
Under a sky
Of pure, dazzling light,
And saw small flowers
Shining with such radiance –
All washed with colour,
Brilliance and light.

I saw how like a vision
Was the landscape,
Ablaze with such intensity
Of light,
And breathed a breath
Of such astounding fragrance –
Of pure earth –
All spotless, all delight.

To see that rare
And so radiant vision,
To smell that fragrance,
Breathe its pure breath,
To see that light –
So dazzling in its radiance,
Was worth the dark and dangerous
Paths of death.

Yes, it was worth
The journeys of great darkness,
So many journeys
Through the blackest night –
For just to See –
For one brief, shining moment –
Was all of life –
Its meaning
And its quest.

I was able to write of this experience of light
only because of the dark and hard experiences
– that forged the vision.

I Know a Stream

I know a stream
All shining and all dazzling
And I can hear it singing,
It blinds me with its light
So all illumining
Transcending fair diamonds of kings !

And standing there
So quietly bestowing
Their matchless fragrance
Of a newborn Spring,
Are lilac flowers
Opening and blossoming
Amid the radiant song of hidden wings.

Yes, I know a stream
All a' dazzle and a' gleam –
With starlight
And moonlight
White sunlight,
And all my memoried dreams.

Peace

World so weary
So weary with waxing and waning
Bowing beneath such weights
Of intolerable strain,
Wait, while the sun
Seems now to be only waning,
Wait, till the stars stand still
And the shy moon reigns.

Right at the apex
Of Heaven's far infinite height
Shines, out of sight,
Such a sweet abundance of light;
Wait world till peace
A peace so sure and unfailing
Shines down
On your wasted and worn and care-ridden face.

Then, like a garden in bloom,
Like the first fair garden
Shall shine
All your fair and shimmering innocent grace:
Like a springtime,
A springtime forever returning
Fair world you shall shine
In the infinite garment of peace.

1988

Love and Light

Shall Love and Light be overcome
Now darkness broods
And drowns the sun
And all of man's bright sands have run –
Shall these fair stars
Drown, with the sun ?

It shan't be so –
For from that sky behind the night
I heard the song of Love and Light:
'Though darkness broods with wings of night
It can't shut out our shining light':

For we are stronger and more bright
And blazing still despite the night;
Though dark is strong,
Both Love and Light
Shall long outlive
The darkest night !

Anemones

Anemones at Christmas bloomed
And their loveliness
Enriched the room
With colours of such vividness
That shone with such unearthliness –
How rich we were
To be so blest
By all their radiant loveliness.

Radiant Earth

O' wondrous radiant world out there
Where your blue globe spins in the crystal air
Would that we all could kneel in prayer
At your wonder that turns in the shining air.

For all your wondrous raiment fair
Is woven on luminous looms of air –
All essence of loveliness
Womb of all life
Is woven on golden threads of light.

But now it is night in the world out there
And the radiant earth carries our despair,
But still she lies quietly dreaming there
Weaving her gifts in her golden hair –
But now with her loveliness locked away
With her beautiful dreams
Of her summer's day.

Broken

With broken wings
My spirit sings
With broken heart
It prays,
But still its sight
Stays true
And unafraid.

White-Winged Bird

My soul is a white-winged bird
Whose shy, shy breast
Is precious and of amethyst;
And of amber
Are its eyes
And full of light
And yet its sight
Can penetrate the night;
Of pure rose its heart
Mirroring the all-enduring sun;
And its spirit strong
As it beats its wings
Takes flight and sings
At Heaven's gate –
Remembering.

Brave Bird

Shy sweet bird
With crimson breast
Where have you built
Your tender nest –
Under the fragile leaves
Of Spring
Near a nest of down
Do you sit and sing ?

Bird with the bravest
Heart I know
I've seen you sing
In deepest snow,
And braver still
I've seen how you
Still trust us –
Unworthy few !

In Time to Come

In time to come
My lost one
In some far distant place
I feel you will remember
My pure and lovely face.

I feel you will remember
When all the world is night
My small and shining spirit
That made your world so bright.

I feel you will remember
The valiant friend in me
Who risked her life
And bore your strife
And sailed your stormy sea.

Yes, in the far, far distance
In some sweet place we knew,
I feel you will remember
How my soul gave light to you.

It is Night

It is night.
No star in sight,
No light.

It is cold.
No warmth exists,
No hope.

It is Spring.
And though birds sing ,
No sun they bring –

But still I sing.

The Blackbird's Song

The liquid song
The Blackbird sings
Bestirs my soul
Its song to sing.

The fluting melody
He sings
Is pure and born
Of earth's first Spring.

O' sweetest bird
With soul so bright
Bestir my soul
To sing with light !

The Light of Paradise

It was the light of Paradise
That shone on us that day
We saw the glow of Heaven's face
In all the world's display.

In the gold and silver slender trees
All dressed with such delight
And in the wild roses' tender cups
Brimful of Heaven's light.

In the tender-blossomed Apple trees
Whose fragrant blooms
Were feasts for bees,
And in all the tender grasses there
All interlaced with flowers fair.

It was the light of Paradise
That shone on us that day :
But now I wish
That pure bright bliss
Had borne my soul away.

With apologies to Thomas Hood !

Luminous Butterflies

Luminous butterflies
Blue as the sea
Spun by a Being
Of mystery.

Luminous butterflies
Blue as the sky
Fashioned by Angels
Of Paradise.

Luminous butterflies
Blue as the air —
Beings of Paradise
As holy as prayer.

And Still I Love —

And still my 'childhood's' flowers
Light the fields,
And still their radiance
Heaven's wonder yields.

And still all fragrant flowers
Their beauties bring –
Like many maidens
Born of earth's pure spring.

And still that dazzling light
Embraces me
And leaves me wondering
At its mystery.

And still the sacred trees
Their silence sing ,
Like many doves
Unfolding many wings.

And still the tiny birds
Sing endlessly
Their pure songs
To lift the weight on me.

And still I love,
Much more now, all of these:
O' shining skies and fields
And radiant trees.

The Garden

In a garden of roses
When Spring filled the air
We planted these flowers
And bowers so fair.

In a garden of roses
We sowed seeds of love
Which we watered with innocence
Rained down from above.

Then in the garden of roses
Grew sweetness and joy,
With the grace of a young girl
And the pride of the boy.

But in the garden of roses
Asleep in the sun,
Lay the serpent of Eden
His moment now come.

For in every fair garden
No matter how pure
Sleeps the serpent of evil
Whose presence endures.

For the fable, the fable,
That was told long ago,
Repeats its old story
Of beauty and woe.

And the garden, the garden,
Stays ever the same:
With the roses and the serpent,
And the beauty and the pain.

Light

It is the everlasting light
That so enchants
My mortal sight;
It is its sheer unearthliness
So dazzling in its loveliness
And all its lovely changing hues
That with delight
My soul imbues.

Eden – Long Ago

See how the fields
Wave their fragrant hands –
Bowers of Eden
Of Eden long ago.

See how the grasses
Sing out to us
Sing out their loveliness –
Visions of Paradise
Of Paradise long ago.

How simple then
How pure and innocent
How bright that new beginning
And light the day
How far the vision
And high and born of light
How far we came
To this so dark a night.

But see the sun
How still its radiance gleams
On all the fields
Of all our broken dreams
And see its light
How dazzling and how bright
And how it still
Illuminates the night.

So sing, sing out
Bright fields of Paradise
Let all your beauty live
Eternally
And let your fragrance rise
Forever to the skies –
O' live, O' live
Remembered Paradise.

The Elephants

All of the elephants
So noble and beautiful
Fewer and fewer
Their numbers became
For all of the elephants
Were slaughtered
For ivory and money and gain.

Now all of the elephants
So noble and beautiful
Are ghosts of our memory
And Africa's Plain;
Yet all of the elephants
So noble and beautiful
Will haunt the bare desert
With 'our' loss and their pain.

Candles in the Dark

Like candles in the dark
They shine
Like candles in the dark,
Who bear oppressions
Heavy cross
Who pay the price
Who know the cost,
Who walk the shadow-side of life
Who choose the dark
The war, the strife;
Who stand unbowed
Unbought, unsold,
Who live in light
Yet dwell in cold,
Who know the fear
The pain, the price
Yet live their lives
Through sacrifice:
Like candles in the dark
They shine
Like candles in the dark.

Returning Spring

Light luminescent
And nature pubescent
And soft the returning
The blossoming Spring;
Brighter and brighter,
Lighter and lighter:
O' gleam immemorial
What beauty you bring.

Wings iridescent
And songs liquescent
And pure the returning
Unfurling of wings;
Sweeter and sweeter
Deeper and deeper:
O' songbirds of Eden
What music you bring.

Air incandescent
And sweet the earth's essence
As it seeps into petals
Unfolding with Spring –
Fairer and fairer,
Rarer and rarer:
O' flowers of the wilderness
What wonder you bring.

But where is the weaver
Who weaves with such wonder
World so miraculous
Woven with light ?
Air, earth and fire
All I desire:
But veiled is the 'Vision'
By the beauty of night.

Storm's End

I never felt such stillness
In the air
As on this day,
The fallow fields
Lie silent and serene
And all the air
Is lit with Heaven's gleam
As if last winter's storm
Had never been.

So hushed, so still,
The very earth seems sleeping
The lake lies still
Its surface all of light
Where blossom swans
Like mystic water flowers
As air and earth and sky
Defy the coming night.

Soul Child

Hold my hand
My small hand
Walk with me
This alien land.

Watch small soul
Long with me
Through the darkness
Shrouding me.

Pure you are
As wild bird
And pure your songs
As singing birds.

Bright your innocent
Soul in me –
May it live –
For eternity.

Small your being
Bright as sun,
Stay as whole
As three, in one.

Crushed my being
Bruised and torn –
Let us both
Be now reborn.

Live bright spirit
Live in me
With my soul
Be one with me.

Brave small soul
Strong small heart
Pure sweet Spirit
All thou art.

The Berried Tree

The light was golden
By the berried tree
When a bird of flame
Sang out to me;

And the soul of the bird
Was full of light
And his song so pure
And he burned so bright.

But though the light
Was golden there
Shadows shadowed the
Shining air.

But the beautiful tree
Was dressed in light
And its golden boughs
Bore berries bright.

But though the berries
Were wine with bloom
And their tiny beads
Breathed a sweet perfume,
My spirit backward looked
While there
For the pure white flowers
That had blossomed there.

For I remembered
The tree in flower
And a golden time
And a golden hour
When my spirit bloomed
In the heart of me
As the flowers had bloomed
On the berried tree.

But time and the
Heavy hand of Fate
Had felled the tree
And locked the gate

And my soul was sad
In the heart of me
For the innocence slain
By the berried tree.

But still the bird
Sang out to me
In the golden boughs
Of the berried tree,

And still all innocence
Shone for me
In the bird and his song
And the berried tree.

1989

Christmas Eve

Christmas Eve
And suddenly
Such a singing
Surrounded me
As every bird
In every tree
Sang its soul
Into melody.

While I so mute
So grounded here
Could only lend
A listening ear.

Until their song
So flooded me
With such astounding
Harmony –

That then my
Boundless soul
Took wing,
And with those birds
Began to sing !

– It did happen on a very mild December 24th !

74

Loss

O' I would walk
In fields of flowers
As once I did
In childhood's hours,
And I would feel
Secure there
As once I did
When fields were fair.

For fields no longer
Shine with flowers
No longer hold
My childhood's hours,
For man has cast
Such shadow there
That I no longer
Wander there.

The Sea Lavender

Where the winds blow
And the white waves break
By a sun-swept wind-swept sea,
In small blue pools
Like dazzling jewels
The lovely sea lavender blooms.

O' by what great hand
In this sun-swept land
And by what majestic soul,
With such infinite care
Planted just there
These beautiful pools of blue ?

What radiant hand
In this wind-swept land
What consummate mind could dream
Of weaving just there
From the gossamer air
These dazzling flowers so blue ?

O' small blue pools
O' dazzling jewels
With your feet in the salty sea,
May you long bloom there
In the sun-swept air
By the edge of the blue blue sea.

Golden Flowers

Golden flowers
How you haunt me
There at my
Nativity,

Shining, shining
In the sunlight –
Childhood's epiphany.

For your fragrance
All about me
Was the breath
Of Paradise,

Paradise was
All about me
As I knelt
In adoration,

Seeing then the
Hem of Heaven
In your dancing, dancing,
Dancing !

My Will, My Will

I write in blood
Drawn by the flood of night
That's drowned
Our dreaming world.

All's lost
All life laid waste
That shone so bright
When angels
Walked the earth in light.

All kill
And kill and kill and kill –
'My will, my will,
Not thine be done.'

And drowned the sun
Man's sands all run;
My will, my will
Not Thine
Is done.

What Now Remains ?

Fair shining fields
And trees of singing birds
Where heaven's innocence is heard,
Bright stars, pale moon and sky
And all that light I'm dazzled by –
How all is now undone and all unsung.

Where blows the wild rose
In secrecy ?
Where flies the dazzling bird
And where its nest ?
Where stand tall trees together
In great gatherings
With all their graceful arms
Encompassing
That endless song
And all that tender fluttering ?

Where sings, who brings
On shining wings
That fragrant blossoming
Full of the bloom of flowers
And sunlit seas,
Whose soft incense invaded me
Almost imperceptibly ?

O' rain, O' radiant sun
O' shining stars –
What now remains unscarred
Of all your great majesty
And what, unmarred ?

1990

It is Innocence

It is innocence
That opens wide
The windows of the soul;

Clear calm state
That smiles on daisies:
Tender – eyed simplicity;

Sweet remembered
Deep remembered
Infant light.

The Sweet Birds Sing

The birds sing
The sweet birds sing
Into the storm
That carries the Spring.

And the trees flower
Blossom and leaf
Into the sun
That buries my grief.

And the earth chimes
Dances and sings
Dazzles my soul
With the rite of Spring.

The Little Hawthorn Trees

See the little Hawthorn trees
In their lovely summer dresses
And fragrant flowing tresses
Standing by the little river
Where the birds their wings a'quiver
Are singing, singing, singing,
And where all the air is ringing –

And where lovely wild white flowers
Bloom in hidden secret bowers,
Where the sunlight gleams so brightly
And the moon its radiance nightly
Guides the tiny halting footsteps
Of the lonely child Man
Who has lost his sense of kinship
In his brief bedevilled span.

But the fragrance on the breeze
From the little Hawthorn trees
And the lovely wild white flowers
Hidden in their secret bowers
Still possess their magic powers
To quite steal my soul away.

The Sleeping World

I keep watch
A night watch
Through the dark
That's drowned the world,
For the world sleeps,
Sleeps and never wakes,
Never dreams.

When will it wake
And waking, dream;
When will it see
The world I see
The world awakening,
Where night wakes
And waking, sings ?

When will it see
The Light I see,
The singing Light
That breaks through
Our sleeping –
Where innocence, sings ?

When will it see
The birds of light
In leaves of light
The world in flower
The flowering light ?

And all, all,
Just out of sight
To their sleeping night,
Night without light
Without dream,
Eternal night.

The Trespassers

Because we trespassed
Trespassed here –
See now the landscape
Dark and sere.

Because we faltered
Faltered here –
See how the shining's
Disappeared.

Because our falling
Fell so far –
See now the heaven's
Falling stars.

Because the serpent
Dazzled us
With all his dreams
Of avarice

And all his dupes
Of power and vice –
We lost the gift
Of Paradise.

Moment of Roses — for Rosie

There was a moment
In the sunlight
Where the lovely
Wild rose bloomed
Walked sweet Rosie
Talked sweet Rosie
With my soul
That afternoon.

And how your soul
Danced, sweet Rosie,
How your spirit
Lit the day,
Where the lovely
Wild roses
Danced with you
That summer's day.

And in that moment
Danced the sunlight
With the lovely
Wild rose,
Where the soul
Of an angel child
Danced with the soul
Of the world – grown old.

But in that moment
Still the Springtime
Still the Summer
Blossomed sweet,
There where the lovely
Wild roses
Danced with the sunlight
At their feet !

Soul's Country

Seeing its future
My soul withdrew;

Terror seemed
To stand tall
As did the darkness.

Trembling,
My soul took strength

And found a way
Through the darkness,

And found the sunlight
And singing birds,

Sweet trees
Their dappled leaves
Dancing,

And many creatures
Small and warm

And incredible flowers,
And silver streams
Where blue birds fished.

And there,
In soul's country,
Found great quiet
Great serenity,

Places for the soul
For the spirit
To shelter,

And sacred green places
Within
Patterned with sunlight
And enduring joy.

For it remembered
Things past –
A golden enchantment,

Found a knowledge
Of patterns,

A knowing
That All
Is 'other' than this –

And that 'That other' –
Is bliss !

Not of the Night

Not of the night
I'll tell,
Not of the night,
Though I have
Walked through Hell,
I'll tell of the light.

Light that is born
Of night,
Light that transcends
The night,
Light that transfigures
Night:
Light of the night.

Little Lizard

Little lizard basking
In the soft September sun
Princely in your self-possession
Ancient as the sun.

In accord with all
About you
In your coat of amber-gold
Set with precious stones
Of diamond,
Amber, green as emerald.

There you sat
In princely splendour
In the last
Of summer's gleam
Total in your self-possession –
Suddenly
As in a dream.

Morning Suns

O' in the morning sun
How we shone
How Eden burned
How our song rung !

And you like the sun
And fair as an oak —
With your leaves
Tender as a Hare's ears —
How they sheltered me
In their green-gold light.

While I,
Shy as a leveret
And as innocent as a dove,
Stepped lightly
Into that newborn day
And slept
And dreamed.

And my tree
Sprung then
Slender as light
With leaves that shone
O' like another sun.

And the trees flowered
And the birds
Filled our branches
And built their nests
And sang,
And summer rose
Like a dove in glory.

And we slept
And we dreamed
In our summer's light
Like gods in Eden.

Two children were we
For innocence was ours
And it opened the casements
Of our souls,

And we saw
Heaven then –
Some semblance
Of its glory –
And it shone
In our dream
Like the sun.

1991

I Was a Garden

I was a garden
Where Paradise bloomed
And where white doves sang
By the light of the moon.

And I was a limb
Of the world's great tree,
Where the wild birds sang
With the wind's harmony.

Now the world's waves rise
On my every side
And the sky shuts out
The moon –
And the seas are so deep
And their waters unsweet –
And the wild tree
No longer blooms.

For the tree in the garden
Breaks in the wind,
And the birds,
Where the tree bloomed,
No longer sing –

But I was a garden
Where Paradise bloomed -
And the birds' song
Was my song –
And the blossoms –
My bloom.

Elegy

Here shall my spirit haunt
And here shall it stay
In the fragrant leaves
Where the wild birds play
In unending day.

And here shall my wild soul sing
And here shall it rest
By the shadowy stream
Where the white swan nests
In unending quest.

And here where innocence dreams
Shall my soul dream
Remembering
When all the air
Was white with blossoming;
Yes, here shall I rest and sing
And fold my wings.

See the Spring

See as Winter
Beckons Spring –
Such a sudden
Blossoming

For where the earth
Lay dark and sere –
Shining flowers
Now appear

And where woods
Stood dark and bare –
Silken tassels
Deck their hair,

While around
Their sturdy feet
Radiant flowers
Blossom sweet.

O' see the sun's
Enamelling
See its shining
Diadem,

As the birdsong
Fills the air –
See the newborn
Everywhere !

Water of Life

Where in this wasteland
Is water to be found ?

Seek not in barren ground
Nor in the forest
All around;

Open not the holy books -
It is not there.

You must endure the wasteland
Then ascend –
Walking through ice and fire,

And at your journey's end
Then apprehend within you

For only there
Will you find water –

In your own soul's flowering.

'The Kingdom of Heaven
Is within You'
Said the Christ.

The Vanished Land

I love this land
This little Eden land
Of flowering fields
And swiftly flowing streams
Where blue birds fish
From water's hallowed gleam.

Its sacred trees
And shining pure streams
Where Paradisal birds
Sing songs of dream
Are desecrated now
And vanishing
And shall become
But songs that poets sing.

And they shall sing
And bless with tender hands
And shall remember
Where the wild birds sang
In wild woods
Where holy rivers ran –
Remembering in dream
The vanished land.

The Mirrored Dream

And if I say
That all our days
Are shadows
Cast by the sun
Of some great distant dream,
And all that seems so new
And dressed in wonder
Is but an image
Mirrored on a screen.

And if I say
That all our lives
Tho' sunlit,
And all we long for
Dream about and seem,
Is but a pale reflection
Of the wonder
Of the long-lost fable
Mirrored in our dreams.

Then what I say
Is Truth
And so eternal
Since Adam fell with Eve
So long ago –
For there remains
No trace of our lost splendour –
But only shadows
Images and dreams.

A Small Bird Sings

Dark is the forest
And there no singing
No sound,
Only silence rebounds
With its echoing, echoing.

But sudden within
A small bird sings
Shakes its white wings –
Then all of a sudden
The whole world
Is dazzling !

Roundelay

Take my darkness
And my light
For both of these
Are my delight.

Take my winter
And my Spring,
In my soul
Life's mirroring.

Take my laughter
And my pain
All life turns
And turns again.

And take my love
And let it sing –
Summer, Winter,
Autumn, Spring.

1992

Echoes

All's past –
The sunlight and the song,

And the pure, pure love
That shone
All the day long;

And now only echoes sing –
Sing their sad song.

Bringer of Gifts

I will adorn with flowers
The ravished land
And set the birds to sing
Unlock the frozen roots of forests
And all their blossoming.

Then shall I gild
And then enamel
All things that I have made,
That you may see
In mystery
My Mirrored Soul unveiled.

Is This the Place?

'Is this the place
This dark, dark place
And this my race ?'
My soul replied –
'It is.'
And hid her face.

For what of the
Treacherous land
And the shifting sands
And all the murderous hands ?
'You shall be quite safe.'

So then
When the rains began
My spirit sang
Of all the beauty
Of this shining land –
Despite the night
And the shifting sands
And all the murderous hands.

Flowers of Light

See the fields
Of swaying poppies
See their chaliced
Cups of light,
See the banks by
Shining waters –
Laced with fragile
Flowers of light.

There together,
Spring and Summer,
Such a feast
Of heaven's light,
Fields and hedgerows
Woods and meadows
Incandescent –
With flowers of light.

Fair Earth

Fair Earth —
How your loveliness
Lights me —
How your Beauty
Delights me —
Lights my soul.

How your innocence
Charms me,
Calms me —
Stays my departing —
Stays my Soul

All of you keeps me —
Steeps me in wonder —
Stills the cruel thunder —
Keeps my Soul —

From the teeth
That would tear me
From the hands
That would wound me
From the minds that would kill me —
Kill my Soul

Let your loveliness
Fill me
Let your innocence
Still me
Stay my departing —
Still my Soul,
Stay.

And I Shall Remain

And I shall remain
In the shining sun
And the radiant stars
Till all days are done.

And I shall be seen
Where the wild rose blooms
And where sacred trees
Breathe their sweet perfume.

And I shall be heard
In the wild bird's song
And the flowing streams
Till all time is done.

So shall I remain
In all things sublime
One leaf of the Tree
Till the end of Time.

This to be my epitaph.

The Golden Land

The golden sun
Now lights
The golden leaves
And golden birds
Now sing
From golden trees
Where golden flowers
Are thronged
By golden bees
All feeding on
The golden-nectared seeds.

For all is gold –
The sun,
The shining seas,
The winds that blow,
The pure air we breath,
And there remains
The endless mystery
Behind whose veil
There shines the Deity.

Storm Birds

Seeing,
In the morning sun,
All the bright birds
At play,
I marvelled at how
Undismayed were they
After that long, long
Storm-tossed yesterday.

Seeing them then
So wind-blown
And rain-lashed,
I thought
How brightly fearless
Were they
On that dreadful
Darkening day.

Would that I could then
Be as they
All bright- plumaged
When gales of hell
Fill my own dark day:

And would, that I could then,
Fly like them —
Away.

After a severe storm in October 1992

1993-2003

Fire Bird

Suddenly there
The bird
Dazzling
In the morning air –
Descended
As from Paradise.

Its being burned
Flamed
Lovely
As sunlit seas –
Lit
By the hidden fire.

Magical bird
What mystery
Brought you here ?

Crowned by the sun
And wearing
The sky's bright morning –
You must be
Heaven-spun.

Spring

See the Spring
As she advances
With her fragrant
Wayward glances.

See her feet
And how she dances,
Treading flowers
As she advances.

See her hands
Are laden branches,
Strewing flowers
As she advances.

I Said to the Sun

I said to the sun –
'Why shine ?
For here
All is dark and decay
And swift decline.'

And I said to the trees
'Why grow ?
For though you are
Tall today –
You will fall
Tomorrow.'

And then to the flowers –
'Why bloom ?
Your beauty but lasts
For a morning –
And is gone
By noon.'

And again to the light –
'Why shine ?
Your radiance
Is wondrous to see –
But then
It is night.'

Then the trees
And the flowers
And the light
Turned round
And smiled at me –

'Why stay ? –
Because we are Love
Is why we stay;
And though we seem
To last but a day –
We ever, stay.'

'For all is a round'
Said they;
'No thing decays –
But ever- stays.'

Dream

There where the trees
Are just in leaf
Where the sunlight
Streams
On the sweet earth's breast
Shall I take my rest
And sleep among flowers so blue.

Where the sunlight streams
Where the sweet earth teems
With a life so rare, so true,
Shall I sweetly stand
And clasp the hand
Of the fragrant flowers so blue.

Yes, there shall I rest
On the sweet earth's breast
And there shall I sleep, and dream,
Of the sun's great light,
And the flowers so bright
That live in a world of dream.

Innocence is Starlike

Innocence is starlike
And the perfection of wholeness,
And its presence is
As a pure stream
Bubbling with light;

For gaiety is in its dancing
As it moves with a grace to be seen
Swaying in the leaves
Sunlit and starlit.

And it is flower-like
In its essence
And full of a fragrance
That is heaven-like
In its sweetness
And as balm to the soul.

And it burns with a clear radiance
That ascends steadily
Towards the sun,

And it is full of
A tenderness
Whose touch is
As the breath of a bird -
Full of love.

And it lacks nothing,-
For it is in possession
Of everything -
It is God.

The World's Wound

Dark, dark
Is the human heart
A sea of dark –
A wasteland.

What moves therein,
What, if anything, lives ?

I can see nothing -
Nothing but the dark.

What caused such death
Such darkness ?

'Loss of love,'
Someone answered,–
'Loss of love,

That is their wound
The world's wound
That caused the death within.

Love to give
And given love –

Their loss

Is why
Their souls cry –

Cry in the dark,

And will
Until
This world ends.'

The Pheasants' Field

Low Sun –
But gold deep –
Shone on the field
Where pheasants
In orient plume,
Fed on the fallen grain
Of summer's feast.

And still was the land,
And still my soul
So still,
And full of the presence
Of peace –
And soft was the fall
Of Summer's golden lease.

And glad was my heart
My soul, so glad,
As it gathered, as the pheasants,
The gleaming grains
From fields of peace.

– from a field next to woods;
Trenley Park Wood near Fordwich, Autumn 1993.

Innocence

Innocence stands
On the shining land
Clasping flowers
In her hands :

When shall we understand
The shining land
Where innocence stands –
Flowers now falling
From her hands.

Never such Light

Never such beauty breaking
In the morning Sun,
And never such light –
As the sweet earth awakened
From the immaculate night.

Wild swans were descending
In the innocent air –
Alighting as flowers
And blossoming there.

While the choiring of birds
Rang pure in the leaves,
And the fragrance of flowers
Was sweet on the breeze,
And the eyes of my soul, Knew,
They never had seen
Such wonder awakening
Out of the dream.

*– Written after seeing yet again but forever
new, Chilham lakes on an April morning.*

Suspended Time

The rain-drenched air
Was sweet, was sweet,
Bright shone the flowers,
Each new-born leaf,
Bright butterflies
Bejewelled the air
Sweet rapturous song
Was everywhere.

It seemed we were
In Eden there
For earth's 'first flowers'
Were Everywhere
And time, it seemed,
Suspended there -
For God's bright face
Was everywhere.

— an April afternoon in a country lane
at Crundale, near Wye, in 1998.

The Clouded Yellows

The Summer's Sun
Has bleached ten million grasses
To pure bone
And bone-white earth
Has given birth to butterflies.

The powdered pigment
Of their wings
Is dust of earth and sky,
These summer grasses sing
With tiny creatures;
They bask in light
Their energy renewed.

– And suddenly,
In summer's ceaseless brilliance,
– Bright wings of Gold,

An endless praise,
A litany,
Epiphany,
Of you.

*– inspired by many visits to the Lydden,
Temple Ewell Downs during the late
summer of 2000 – a wonderful summer,
blessed by the appearance of many Clouded
Yellow butterflies.*

Love Is Eternal

Be with us
Through our life's travail
To the gleam
Of bright new morning,

Who ever we are
What ever we do
Love is eternal.

Butterflies

'They seem pure sunlight'
rising through delicate air
with such grace:
See how they soar –
Soar ever upwards and from us –
Vanishing points of light
In infinite space.

– on Ann's birthday card to me,
– November 2001.

I am in the Rainbow
I am in the Lifeforce
I am the Love
That is within – and without.

This verse was received from Ann, by Karin Page,
during a spiritual workshop in June 2003.

ACKNOWLEDGEMENTS

I HAVE received much encouragement and support during the time that this book of poems has taken to reach fruition. A great deal of that encouragement has come from those with deeply felt spiritual convictions and I am extremely grateful for this support.

There must, however, be one exception to this collective acknowledgement. In the early days of its preparation my principle asset was determination. But that alone would not have sufficed and I am indebted to my brother Brian, not only for his support and encouragement, but more particularly, for his practical and remarkably enthusiastic assistance. Without any prior experience and armed initially only with his computer skills he has methodically assembled all the material which I have cumulatively provided him with and brought the book to the point where it was ready for printing. During its preparation Ann has more than once observed that the three of us have been working together on it.